How to Create your own Crystal Grids

A Step by Step Guide

by Kristi Hugs

Disclaimer:

The information contained in Crystal Basics 101 is not meant to replace diagnosis and treatment by a qualified and licensed medical practitioner. ALL recommendations herein contained are derived from article research, various crystal reference books and intuition. No expressed or implied guarantee as to the effects of their uses can be given nor liability taken.

What is a Crystal Grid?

A Crystal Grid is simply the placing of crystals in a pattern chosen by you, based on a specific intent/purpose/goal.

How do they work?

The crystals you select have specific energy vibrations/frequencies. The pattern you chose to lay the crystals out in, be it a template or free form, are a way to direct that energy. The crystals, the template and your intention for this grid all work in combination towards this common goal by merging the energies, raising the vibration and expanding the energy to make the space conducive

What are Crystal Grids used for?

Anything! You can create a crystal grid for healing, love, abundance, success, peace, support for a friend or loved one, dreams and dreaming, astral travel, meditation, compassion, protection, safe travel.....the list is literally endless!

Let's take this Step by Step.

Step One - Intent or Intention

Ask yourself what will this grid specifically be for? I personally prefer to use a single, very specific intent.

You may decide to use more than one intention at a time. Make sure that it complements the other. (For example: a grid for both love and healing.)

Try to keep it focused. Too many intentions (intents) in one grid may create a weaker, less focused energy. Think of a time when you tried to be in too many places all at the same time. Your energy is scattered and less focused. The same goes for a grid.

Sit quietly for a moment. Find your center or that quiet place where you are completely focused and still. Be as specific and clear on your intent as you can be.

Remember, the grid will be a tool to amplify these thoughts, feelings and/or intent, so you want to state your intention with absolute clarity.

"It is my intention that this crystal grid be created to assist with……."

Write down some goals and/or intentions that you would like to use later as a basis for creating a crystal grid.

Step Two – Location

The next thing you will need to decide is where will this grid be located? Will this be outdoors in your garden or indoors on an altar? Maybe you would like to place the grid under your bed to enhance your dreaming or astral travel adventures.

A sacred space, such as your healing room or meditation area would be very conducive to gridding. You can even grid your home, inside and out! The possibilities are endless and opened to your imagination.

The idea will be to place the grid in an area where the crystals surrounding it would not be disturbed. *But please, take this to heart– if the crystals are disturbed?? DO NOT be upset!! Things happen. Simply replace the crystals in their designated areas, re-connect and activate the grid, and go about your day worry free.*

Write down some locations where you would love to create a crystal grid.

Step Three - Size

There are many grid sizes and truly, this is up to you.

At a recent crystal bowl ceremony, a grid was set up to accommodate a person in the center while others formed a huge outer circle around the one in the middle. It was quite a sight to see!

You can make a grid small enough to sit on a windowsill or a nightstand.

You can create a crystal meditation grid large enough to sit comfortably in the middle of.

Build a healing grid under your massage or healing table to enhance the energies of a healing session.

Small, Medium, or Large ~ this is a personal preference and should be in alignment with your intent.

Templates

Let's talk a moment about templates. What is a template?

A template is a pre-designed shape or layout meant to replicate a specific design (like the flower of life). This template can help to further create a specific energy field.

Your next decision should be--Do you want to use a template as a guide for your grid? Or will you be creating from intuition?

Shapes can help to focus the energy of the intent.

The next few pages highlight some basic shapes you may want to consider.

The Circle/Wheel

The Circle is an ancient and universal symbol of Unity, wholeness, infinity, the goddess and female power. It is the symbol of cosmic unity, "the circle of life", and evolution. The wheel also symbolizes movement the sun, the zodiac, reincarnation and earth's cycles of renewal.

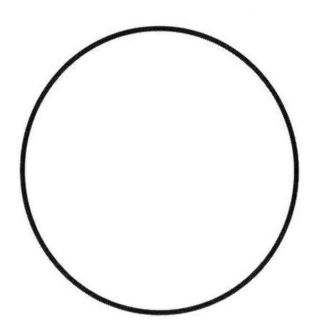

The Square

The Square represents the physical world, stability and sacred Earth.

The Diamond, in this template, is simply a tilted Square. The lines within (forming a cross) represent the four directions. This template can also represent the four elements: Earth, Air, Fire and Water.

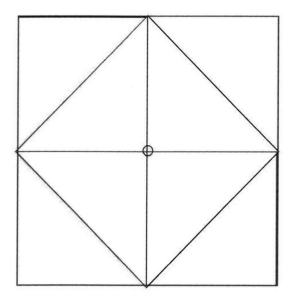

The Infinity Symbol

In ancient Tibet and India, the Infinity symbol will represent perfection, dualism and the unity between male and female.

In the occult Tarot, the Infinity symbol is linked to magic and represents equilibrium or the balance of various forces.

<u>The Spiral</u>

A common shape in nature, the Spiral is an ancient symbol of the goddess, the womb, fertility, feminine serpent force, continual change, and the evolution of the Universe.

Flower of Life

The Flower of Life is considered to be sacred geometry, containing ancient, religious value depicting the fundamental forms of space and time. It is a visual expression of the connections life weaves through all mankind, believed to contain a type of Akashic Record of basic information of all living things. In particular, depictions of the five Platonic Solids are found within the Flower of Life and act as a template from which all life springs.

Tree of Life

The Sephiroth (Sephirot) are central to the Kabbalah. The Sephiroth are usually represented within the "tree of life", a glyph composed of the ten Sephirah and twenty two "paths" (which are represented by the 22 letters of the Hebrew alphabet).

The "Tree of Life" alludes to the interconnection of all life on our planet and serves as a metaphor for common descent in the evolutionary sense. The term tree of life may also be used as a synonym for Sacred Tree.

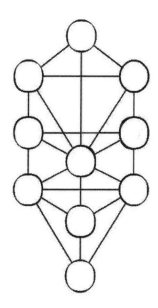

Step Four - Choosing Items for your Grid

Now let's talk about what we are going to put in/on our grid.

I always choose a few things that represent my intent to put in the center of my grid. If it is an abundance grid, I may put an abundance check in the middle, if it is for healing for me, I may put a picture of myself in the middle, if it is for someone else, I would put their picture in the middle and so forth.

Think about what you may want to include in your grid besides the crystals to enhance the intent.

You can also add color energy to your grid- A silk cloth to lay the grid on, flowers, etc.

Make a list of what items you would like to include in your grid.

Crystal Selection

So now, the big question now is............ How will I know what crystals work best?

It is best to use crystals that carry the same energy vibration as your intent.

For instance, if your grid intention is for financial abundance/prosperity, you want to select crystals that carry that energy vibration (mid-range).

If you want to focus and concentrate, you will want to select energy vibrations on the lower end of the scale, the ones that can help to ground and balance you.

To choose your crystals, you may want to do a little research using your favorite crystal book or go online and Google your intent (love crystals, abundance crystals, etc.). Or, you can refer to Table II in the back of this book.

If you work with a pendulum, you can use it to verify that your selections will be the most effective.

Above all else, follow your intuition. Trust that the information you are given is accurate for your grid. Don't question it, just follow and allow.

Quartz Points

Quartz points play a very important role in creating your grid. They are specifically used to direct the energy flow of your grid.

Does it matter how many quartz points? As a rule, I use at least 4 for the outside. They either go on the corners or using the four directions.

I also put three in the center. If you have a specific number that feels right, then by all means, use that number. Just remember, more is not necessarily better.

I often find that I do things in 7's, 10's or 11's. I have no idea why.

I always recommend that if at all possible, there should be standing quartz or other crystal focal point in the middle.

It can be a generator quartz, a natural quartz point (or points) with the bottom smoothed off so it will stand up, a pyramid, a star tetrahedron, a sphere or a free form.

The rest of the points need to be on the outside of the grid (this makes it easier to activate- that will come later). These are just general, loose rules.

Using your intuition to create a grid allows for all kinds of patterns and shapes and free form craziness.

Note: Clear/white quartz points amplify the energies of the intent, but remember Amethyst and Citrine are also types of quartz, so feel free to mix it up if you feel that is what is needed. For instance, adding Citrine points to your

Abundance grid would enhance the energy of abundance and success. You could even alternate Citrine points with clear/white Crystal points to make up your seven points.

Let's look at some point placements for specific energy direction.

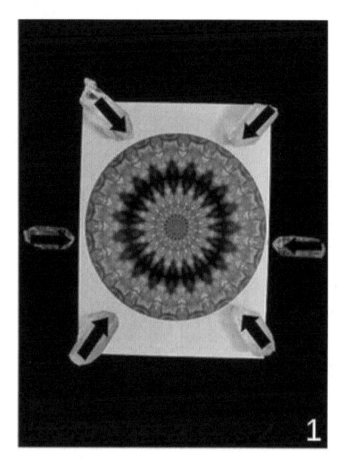

This first example is with the quart points pointing inward. This is for a personal type grid....if you want abundance for yourself, you could put a picture of yourself and a dollar bill or abundance check in the middle. All of the energy of the grid would be directed AT you.

If you are creating a long distance grid for a family member or friend, you want the energy to be sent OUT to them. In this case you would want to point your quartz points out and away from the grid center.

If you are creating a grid for yourself or someone else that may need to infuse the person with grid energy both at home and at work.

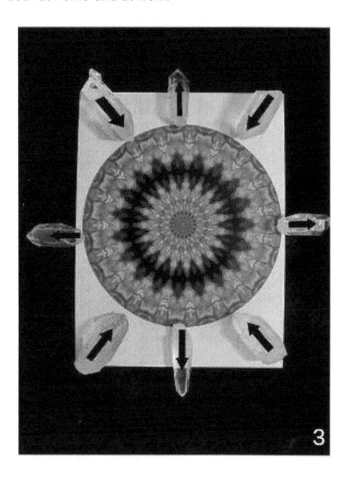

I recommend four quartz points pointing IN to the middle and four quartz points, pointing OUT (sending to universe/work) in an alternating pattern.

Step Five- Clearing your Sacred Space

I recommend that you clear/clean the energy in the area you have chosen for your grid before the actual grid setup takes place. Do not forget to cleanse yourself and the crystals too!

Clearing the energy from a space basically means that any heavy, dense energy or energy that is not conducive to your highest goal/intent of your grid be removed.

Whether you are able to feel this energy or not is ok. It is always a good idea when starting a new project to start with a clean slate, right? Just think of clearing the energy in the same manner—clearing the slate.

Using something as simple as a stick of incense or sage leaf to smudge (cleanse by using smoke— allowing the energy to dissipate like the smoke itself- can be very effective. Don't forget to open the windows to let the smoke and dense energies be released!)

If you are allergic to smoke or scented incense, try using a bell or crystal bowl. Sound is a very effective cleanser.

Another idea is to use a candle/flame that will purify the space.

Use what works best for you.

Step Six – Putting it all together

You and your space are now energetically cleansed and you are ready to begin placing your crystals in the area you have selected for your grid.

Remember, you can lay your grid out in a variety of geometrical shapes or just let your intuition guide you. You may use one of the supplied templates to enhance your intent or go free form. Use whatever you are drawn to.

This is YOUR grid, so the pattern and placement of the crystals is truly up to you. Again, remember, there is NO wrong way to do this. Be creative. Follow your instinct. The creation of a grid can become a form of meditation or creative, self-empowering art.

Activation

After your grid has been created, the last step is to activate it. This is basically a process to connect the crystal energies with your intent.

I have included a picture showing how to activate your grid using the quartz points as your activation points on the following page. Now let's go through it step by step.

First, you will need a single quartz point as the activator. Clear it by using your favorite crystal clearing method.

Once that is done, begin by stating your intent out loud. Using that clear quartz wand, hold it over the main crystal in the center. Point it to the center crystal and then move the wand down to the first crystal making up the outer circle, over to the second crystal and back to the center.

Again, start in the center, out to the second crystal, over to the third and back to the center. Again at the center, to the third crystal, over to the fourth and back to the center. Continue this pattern until you have completed a full rotation.

I always start at the bottom and go in a counterclockwise position, but this is purely a personal preference. Go in whatever direction you feel works best for you. Once you have completed connecting the crystals energy to each other, you may (or may not, again, personal preference) want to state your intent once more, or perhaps an affirmation that has meaning for you and falls in line with your intent.

If any negative thoughts or doubts come up at any time during this process, simply say, "Not in this place." and allow the thought/doubt to dissipate.

This is your sacred space and your sacred grid created by you, a sacred being. Enjoy this process, experiment with different layouts and find what works best for you. Above all, have fun as you learn to create your own personalized crystal grids.

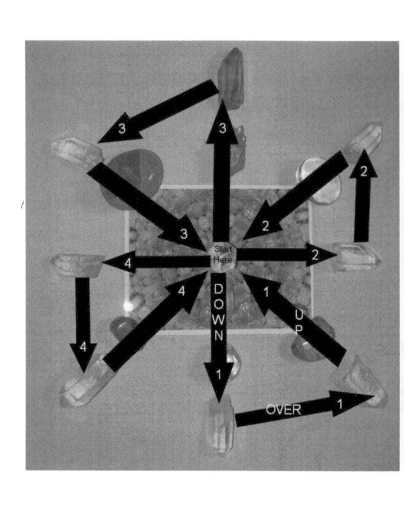

My Crystal Grid Worksheet

What is my intention/goal for this Grid? Where will this Crystal Grid be located? How big will this Crystal Grid be?

What crystals will I use for this Crystal Grid?

What other items will I incorporate into this Crystal Grid?

Do I want to use a template? Or create my own shape for this Crystal Grid?

Have I.........

Chosen a specific Intention/Goal Selected the Crystal Grid Location? Selected the Crystal Grid Size?

Selected the specific crystals I will be using for this Crystal Grid? Selected other items to incorporate into this Crystal Grid? Cleansed the crystals?

Cleansed the space? Cleansed myself? Created the Crystal Grid?

Charged/Activated the grid?

Final thoughts

As you can see, there are a variety of applications with which to utilize your crystals. Here are a few more suggestions.

- Simply adding a tumble to a crystal pouch or medicine bag may suffice.

- Adding a few nontoxic crystals to your bath will help to infuse your body with crystalline energy.

- Adding some crystals or crystal charged water to your plants can aid in growth and health of the plant.

- Grid your property or home to keep the positive energy flowing.

The possibilities are really limitless!

NOTES

<u>NOTES</u>

About the Author

Kristi began her crystal education/journey 20+ years ago and it continues to evolve to this day. Self-taught and in a constant state of study, Kristi shares simple and basic guidance to beginners and advanced crystal enthusiasts alike.

Kristi's published works include: *The Gemstone Healing Guide, A Healing Apothecary* (2005), *The Crystal Council Oracle Cards* (2010), *The Handy Little Crystal List Reference Guide* (2011), *Stepping Stones to Crystal Basics* (2013), *Old Rocks, New Names: Synonyms, Trademark and Marketing Names for Old Favorites and New Finds* (2016), *Crystal Speak-How I learned to communicate with my crystals and how you can too* (2016) *Crystal Basics 101* (2017), *The Crystal Speaks Sessions I* and *The Crystal Speaks Sessions II* (2017) and *The Crystal Council Oracle* (book version of the Crystal Council Oracle Cards) also in 2017.

Kristi lives a quiet, simple lifestyle in Washington State with rescue kitty, Tesha.

Made in the USA
Monee, IL
29 June 2021